Creative Crisis

Creative Crisis

A Spiritual Guide for Mid-Life Men

Donal O'Leary

THE COLUMBA PRESS/TWENTY-THIRD PUBLICATIONS
DUBLIN   MYSTIC, CT

Twenty-Third Publications
185 Willow Street
P.O. Box 180
Mystic, CT 06355
(203) 536-2611
ISBN 0-89622-450-3
Library of Congress Catalog Card No 90-70992

The Columba Press
93 The Rise
Mount Merrion
Blackrock, Co Dublin, Ireland
(01) 832954
ISBN 0-948183-81-0

Preface

If you are a middle-aged man, you may recognise yourself
in these conversations. They describe something of what
happens to us as we live through the decades. We often get
stuck in our development as persons. For a variety of reasons, we stop growing. Our joy, excitement and vision become faded. At a certain stage, depression can set in. This
can be a trying time for many, traumatic for some, challenging for all. Quite often we resist knowing what is happening
inside us, or even admitting that all is not well. Exploring
such personal areas is usually very sensitive and painful.
We prefer not to know, to deny, to laugh it off. But in the
long run, it can destroy us.

Most men are conditioned to deny the reality of the mid-
life crisis. It is a taboo subject. It is often quite difficult for us
to express our emotions, particularly those of loss and grief.
This male condition is itself an added source of inner pain.
When you think about it, there are no customs or rituals or
special sacraments to see us through such seasons of confusion, as there are for the moments of death, reconciliation
and bodily illness.

I wrote this book to help men identify, accept, express
and transcend the huge turmoils of the middle years. But I
wrote it, too, to lift our spirits above the daily routine and
mundane ordinariness that life is made of, and that often
dulls our souls. I tried to paint an exciting picture to glad-

den our hearts by reflecting back to them their own beauty. It is offered as a timely reminder of the loveliness of life, the wonder of creation, the meaning of incarnation.

Creative Crisis calls us to reach our best, to believe in the power of the human heart, to notice the sacred at the centre of everything.

In this story, Paddy made a breakthrough before it was too late. By listening to his own heart and deepest self—his wounded, healing child, and powerful inner voice—he began to grow in ways he never thought possible. Once he overcame his deep-seated resistance to acknowledging how precarious and superficial his life was becoming, he made the first small step of destiny. By opening himself to the power of love, and by trusting in his own heart, he began to let go of useless and crippling fears. Once he became unstuck and began to move forward, a whole new horizon opened up before him. His life assumed a dynamism, a richness and a happiness that he had not dared dream of.

One might be forgiven for thinking that many of the ideas in *Creative Crisis* seem idealistic, many of the claims extravagant, many of the promises unfounded. But they have all been made many times over by the world's wisest and holiest men and women. Jesus Christ was one of these. Yet we are startled at the intensity and hopefulness of their vision when it is set before us in the present tense of everyday language.

Acknowledgments

It was in the womb-like library of Iona Abbey, heavy with tradition and rich in mystery, that I wrote *Creative Crisis*. Through the windows of the renovated monastery, I could see what St Columba looked out on nearly 1500 years ago. Before me, the Sound of Mull sparkled between the Isle of Iona and the Ross of Mull. To the west, beyond Tiree, two thousand miles across the Atlantic, lay the east coast of Canada. And to the south, but out of sight of course, as the legend insists, is the unforgiving coastline of northern Ireland. Every day the view was different because the light kept changing in the translucency and stillness of the island's atmosphere. It was easy to be creative in this place of dreams where creatures and the uncreated dance and play forever. Phillip and Alison Newell, the wardens, welcomed and befriended me, as did all the fine people I met during my days and nights on this holy isle, which still carries the lovely freshness of the beginning of the world.

The Hebrew word for 'dove' is 'Iona'; the Irish is 'colm', latinised as 'Columba'; both words meet at the heart of Columba, or Colmcille, one of Ireland's finest saints and scholars. Where else, then, would I go with my new manuscript but to The Columba Press in Dublin? Seán O Boyle's greeting was so warm that I suspected he knew all along that something like this was going to happen. I thank him for his trust.

I write these words three weeks after my 'handicapped' brother Joseph, another dove of peace, having accomplished his mission here on a wounded, healing earth, returned to the heaven of love from whence he came, to accept his next appointment. Our lives with him made the importance of loving the child within us all so clear— because up to his last gentle smile, as he wonderingly beheld his angels coming for him, he and his inner child were completely one. So much of Joseph's voice is in every conversation in this book.

Kathleen Dillon's conviction that I could write *Creative Crisis* and that it would benefit many spurred me to see the project through. Her wisdom and energy kept my heart up whenever I faltered.

Once again, I acknowledge the help of my family, my Mom, Maura and Mícheál. As often before, they found time to pick up the early pages, persevered in reading them, and offered extremely helpful comments.

Finally, I am indebted to my own inner child. Wherever the conversations that follow are less than true, it is not his fault.

Contents

For what is an Irishman's heart
but his imagination?

George Bernard Shaw

PART 1

Introductions

Paddy at mid-life
Pat=Paddy's childhood self
Patrick=Paddy's inner self

Paddy in Mid-Life

One wintery evening with the fire burning brightly at 52 Iona Avenue, Paddy was not himself. Yet it had been a good day. Earlier, at the Sunday lunch, Eileen had reminded him that it was the twentieth anniversary of their marriage. He always seemed to forget it. In the afternoon he read the Sunday newspaper and then dozed off. After doing the dishes, Eileen liked to write to their two children who had left home for the first time in September. Paddy wasn't much of a hand at writing letters, or at washing for that matter. He wondered why he was still a bit depressed tonight. He shrugged his shoulders and looked at his watch. A few drinks should do the trick, he promised himself. They usually did.

Paddy set off for the pub in his new car. He loved to have a few pints with the lads most evenings, but especially on Sundays. And especially tonight. Kerry had played well today in the National League. Maybe they were on the way back. The lads were always ribbing him about the end of the kingdom's glory. Mick was from Cork; Seán from Dublin.

Paddy was a primary school principal. He was sorry to leave Kerry ten years earlier, but the opportunity came and he took it. Eileen was not so happy about the move. She still wanted to go back home. Only recently she read in the paper about a job opening in Tralee. He told her he wasn't interested. More fun in Dublin, he said. She didn't seem to understand that, he remembered. They had argued. The matter wasn't raised again. The night was wet. He would soon be at the pub. Mick from Cork was always first to arrive. He had a fierce mind for the drink. He was proud of that. Paddy turned on the car radio for the sports report. It was over. Andy O'Mahony was talking to someone about the mid-life crisis in men. What kind of crisis was that, Paddy wondered. Whatever it was, he didn't have it. His current bit of depression would soon pass, he reassured himself. Basically, everything was fine. His job was secure, his marriage sound, his children reasonably successful and his health reasonably good. And with friends like Mick and Seán, how could he even have a hint of a crisis?

Paddy really enjoyed his chats in the pub. Eileen wasn't interested in sports or politics. And she rarely asked him about his work. She never went drinking with him. Mind you, he always refused to go walking with her—he wasn't exactly into nature or even talking about it. In fact, they seldom discussed anything much these days. Now that the children were gone, Paddy wondered how she would cope with a house that was gradually becoming more silent and more empty. When the eldest two were leaving in September, she had tried to talk to him about the pain of letting go. He wasn't sure what she meant. Then she had become involved in a "gardening for therapy" class. He didn't understand this either. Eileen's friend Peggy had signed on for painting and creative writing. It helped them to stay in touch with their feelings, they said. Apparently, they enjoyed being creative. Paddy didn't much go for this. It sounded dangerously like "New Age" stuff from California.

Far from therapy they were reared, he mused. There must be more interesting ways of spending Tuesday evenings. Ten years ago, when they were struggling with small babies and trying to make ends meet, there was no talk about garden-therapy and personal development. They were the quiet women he remembered, thankful to himself and Seán (that's Peggy's husband) for bringing home the money and keeping the wolf from the door during those early difficult years. Mind you, he himself didn't see a great deal of the children then, because he worked late and usually went straight to the pub to unwind with the others.

At this point in his reverie, the warm, welcoming lights of his familiar hostelry came into view. But they did little to lift his spirits.

Neither did the pints and the chasers. It was still raining as Paddy drove home. He was above the limit and below par. The talk had come round to their wives, Eileen and Peggy. (Mick claimed he was too young yet to get married. After he had played the field, he promised, he would pick a nice quiet girl and settle down.) The two women, Seán said, were getting a bit independent. 'Doing their own thing', was how he put it. The nuns had invited the wives round to the convent for a talk by a visiting priest the following evening. It was about something called 'the wounded child'. That was definitely the phrase she used, Seán said. He had asked Peggy what it meant. There was a child within each person, she had said, a kind of voice from the early years, a vague memory, a half-remembered dream. 'The wounded child' referred to the hurts that happened to people during childhood. It was a name given to the damage done to small children by parents and teachers. Even priests and nuns, she said, contributed to the woundedness of young people, with their preaching of an angry God and a roasting hell. Seán and Paddy had agreed that this was nonsense. Maybe it should be stopped. They would talk to their wives tomorrow.

The road was quiet now. The rain had eased off. Like a smile, a quarter moon emerged to transform the stern face of the night. But Paddy never noticed. His uneasiness was giving way to anxiety. Something odd was going on. Why was he feeling down? Was it because of the new turn of events regarding the two women? What was getting into them, he wondered. Why was he resentful about their new interests? Did he feel left out? Was he losing some kind of control? Why did he feel threatened? After all, Eileen was a great wife, pandering to his every wish, at least up to now. Yet this independence had never shown itself before. Maybe they should try to communicate more.

But they never talked about those things—feelings, childhood, special memories and secret hopes. At least he didn't. Maybe he couldn't. Anyway, there was no need. He would find it embarrassing. Somehow it wasn't what men did. Women tended to get over-emotional. Only last week, Eileen had tried to talk about their relationship and about how she felt particularly lonely this autumn, with the two children gone. She would love it if he stayed in more evenings to talk, or took her to a film occasionally. Paddy remembered how he had reacted. First he denied that he was out a lot; then he accused her of nagging; and finally he got angry. It was quite disturbing—their first fight in ages. And he couldn't handle it when she began to cry and turned away. He put it down to 'the change'. He felt better knowing the cause. The lights were off in the house when he pulled into the driveway.

The following week, Paddy was at the doctor's office waiting for Eileen to pick him up. She had persuaded him to go for a check-up, having noticed his anxiety and restlessness. He was worried about something—maybe about dying? His father had died recently, and some of his friends too. Was that why he was so moody? He felt tense and irritable. Yet he played squash every weekend and avoided junk food and salt and fatty bacon. The doctor, who was a bit of a psychologist as well, knew that his general health was fine. Paddy's heart passed all the tests and the quality of his blood was a credit to him. There was no mistake about that. The Dublin doctors had the latest equipment. But why did he say, 'Your hurt is inside'? Doctors don't usually talk like that. He had also asked him about job satisfaction, Eileen and childhood experiences.

Suddenly, snippets of the conversation he had had with Seán that night in the pub flashed across his mind. 'We can carry hurts inside us from childhood.' Much as he resented having anything to do with such new-fangled ideas, Paddy reluctantly allowed his mind to drift back to the days of his Kerry childhood. He was pretty sure he would find no wounds, nor did he wish to. He was right.

They were all golden memories. (Only later would he realise the sad significance of his selected 'golden' moments.) He recalled long days of sunshine in the bog and in the meadows; short winter evenings of homework and snowball fights. There were special moments that stood out—the pair of pearl-handled pistols that were the envy of the Dillon twins next door; the evening that he and Fursy O Brien had their first fight, a bruising marathon-match which he won only when Fursy fainted—and neither of them cried; the spring morning when he snared his first rabbit, making his Dad so proud of him. 'Well done, Pat!' his father exclaimed, 'you'll make a fine hunter yet'; the August day the teacher cycled into the yard with his national test scores. It was the only time he could remember being hugged by his father. His mother was ecstatic. She bought him a bottle of yellow lemonade and some cookies. 'This is only the beginning', she whispered in Pat's ear. 'You will do better and better all the time. Just remember forever the sacrifices your parents are making for you'.

No, he carried few, if any, wounds from those days. Life

was certainly not always easy then, but he grew through the knocks. In sports, too, he learned the tricks of winning. Sometimes you must play the man, not the ball. How quickly he learned to exploit the shady space between fair and foul. And how he lived for each Sunday's victory! His Dad used to boast about him in the pub those nights. Paddy smiled as he reminisced about the midnight celebrations that he too enjoyed in the boys' boarding school he attended, whenever they managed to smuggle in a few bottles of Guinness after a match.

He later went to work in London for a few summers. They were great days altogether. The north Kerry boys stuck together and rarely broke ranks, except when one of them fell in love. They learned not to trust foreigners. They shouted defiantly from a safe distance at British politicians and painted patriotic slogans on empty walls. Overall, they learned that life was safer at home; there was less risk and challenge. It was at home that they all eventually settled down.

Eileen telephoned the doctor's office to say she was held up in town. No sweat. He would enjoy the walk home. It would clear his mind. Paddy was aware that this was no ordinary week. His dissatisfaction and mild depression were now more acute; he was experiencing a new kind of resentment over Eileen's efforts to deal with her emotions and enrich the quality of her life; his body didn't feel right, in spite of the positive check-up—too much tension in it. He was drinking more and enjoying it less; and he found teaching increasingly stressful and unfulfilling. Maybe he should talk to somebody about himself, since all the usual cures were not working. He winced at the thought. It went against the grain. But like confession (before he stopped going) he didn't have to tell all; just enough to give the general idea; nothing heavy. No, definitely nothing heavy.

But talk to whom? His mother was dead, as was his

father. He could never talk to his father anyway; never felt close to him. He was never sure how his father would react. A fine man, though. Seán and Mick, Paddy thought, were great for talking about the usual stuff—matches and politics and the weather. But they would laugh at him over this— they wouldn't understand. And at this time he couldn't approach Eileen. Things were too raw just now. Anyway, he would be too embarassed—they never discussed that kind of thing. His colleagues at school? He didn't trust them. He didn't understand why, but there was no way he could talk to any of them. He couldn't even go to the parent-teacher meetings when his children were small. Maybe one of the priests could help. But he had long since parted company with 'churchy' people and things. He even felt distinctly uneasy going near the church or meeting a priest on the few occasions that he had to for the children's sake. Feeling downright sorry for himself, he realized that he didn't even have a dog or a cat to comfort him. He could never quite figure out why he was so apprehensive all his life about having pets. Only later would he know the reason.

Pat: Paddy's Childhood Self

We will come back to Paddy later. The last few pages have provided a very brief sketch of his thoughts on certain aspects of his life during these days. They have indicated, too, the manner in which he remembers his childhood. What is noticeable is the nature of his memories of childhood: he recalls only incidents that reinforced the male conditioning of the time—work, winning, achievements, guilt and violence. It is at this point that I wish to offer another version of Paddy's life as a boy. I will tell it as young Pat himself told me. (It was during his summers in England that he lost his child's name and began to answer to Paddy.)

The Child of Wonder

Pat loved the sea. It was a continual source of wonder to him. Still as a tree, he would look at it for hours and become lost in its mystery. In his imagination he sailed everywhere. Each new map of distant shorelines launched him on another voyage. He relived in his wild heart the fierce adventures of the fearless explorers who reached them, named them and drew them. He could feel the tides in his own veins and sometimes when he went swimming, he felt the sea was flowing in him. He respected, trusted and loved the water. Every sea, river and stream had different personalities and played different melodies. At that time, Pat was a small, barefoot mystic. He would sit on a rock and his heart would sing to the sea. And the sea would always play back a lovely, haunting melody.

He loved the wind, too. He was forever listening to the stories it told about its travels over land and sea and through the sky. Sometimes he felt he knew these tales already. By day and by night Pat used to dream that he could fly. When the wind blew he would try to catch it in his outspread coat, skipping and running with it, ready for liftoff. Or he would climb a tall, slender tree that swayed a full half-circle in the storm, clinging like a koala bear to the living branch, feeling in his limbs the rhythm of a universal beat. So intimate was his communion with nature as he rode out the passionate gale on his exulting young ash that Pat and the tree seemed carried away by the same rapture.

Paddy, have you really forgotten that? Pat dumbly wonders. Who built the wall that cut you off from your mystical world—your beautiful, magical world of joy?

As with the water and the wind, so too with the earth and all living things. Pat intensely related to all of nature in one ever-changing paradise of surprises. He was truly a child of the universe. He felt that he was a part of everything. (This feeling is not uncommon in childhood but most of us forget it.) Even the rocks talked to him. He would never pick up the small ones to throw at animals—it would be like hitting himself with his own fist, he thought. But he often skimmed the flat stones over the water of the lake; he knew they all enjoyed that. He was able to sense these things. He noticed so much without even trying. One day he felt sure he saw the mark of a seagull's wing in the air as it spiralled in the wind. Another evening his imagination enabled him to hear the faint music made by insects' wings and at another time he felt the indescribable vibrations of pine needles as he walked through his beloved woods. He never told anyone that on a very quiet day he could hear the tiny tunes from the growing grass not unlike the music that stole into his mind when he looked at the stars through the little window of his bedroom when all the houses and the dogs were asleep and the whole earth belonged to him.

You will have noticed how different is Paddy's version of his young days. Oh Paddy, how could you forget those mornings of play when you felt so loved among the apple trees and the haybarns, delighted with yourself all the time, a local hero on your way home to be honoured yet again for discovering undreamed of variations of wonder and beauty on this planet and (more often) beyond? What could have happened to those visions and dreams? Were they lost? Did someone steal them?

For Pat, natural things were always somehow right, especially where they were not tamed, domesticated or landscaped. He was always escaping to wild places either in fact or in fancy. (Reality was flexible in those days.) His heart moved in the wilderness. Perfect wild beauty matched his perfect wild heart. The sight of distant mountains stirred up familiar longings within him and setting suns echoed a strange sadness in his young spirit. It was more of a loneliness, as though he were disconnected from a deeply distant yet achingly familiar homeland that belonged to another time. The wilderness seemed to call him, to tell him it was still the morning of the world, that everything was still young, that God would be busy for a long time. Pat saw something glorious in wildness and felt he was united with it. As a mirror tells us how we look, he knew himself to be an intrinsic part of nature, a small priest whose vocation it was to reflect back to the wild flowers how lovely they were. He felt they would never know if he did not tell them. The wilderness was never so beautiful as when Pat was around it.

But where did the awful blight that brought the famine to the garden of Pat's heart come from? Who caused the fall from graced vision, when the light was dimmed and the wild spirit was tamed? Who stole Pat's dream of a world empowered by love, the dream that Paddy cannot even remember?

How do we explore these questions more fully? Are there any directions toward clarity? We already know a little about Paddy the adult and Pat the child. Even this sketch makes us aware of the significant change that had taken place at some point in the transition from Pat to Paddy. There is little trace of the mystic, the lover of nature, the imaginative creator in the picture we have of the adult. Unlike Pat, whose only instinct was to go with the flow, to follow his heart and his bliss, Paddy is stuck. He is fearful of change yet anxious about being trapped into a routine lifestyle; he is out of touch with his feelings, yet resisting the very suggestion that this may be so; he is vaguely uneasy about his increasing consumption of alcohol yet unwilling to consider any attempt at self-discipline; he is aware that all is not well 'inside' yet mocks the doctor who told him; he is bored with his work but reluctant to break ranks with his cronies to attend workshops or short courses or to try and analyse and imitate the style of those teachers who impressed and enriched his school days in Kerry. The following brief consideration of some obscured but relevant experiences of Pat may enable us to reach some understanding of the negative forces that left their mark on Paddy.

The Wounded Child

One day Pat came home to find his mother crying. His grandfather had died. He thought his heart would break. Everyone knew how close they were. Always with Pat, Old Paul had shared lovely secrets to treasure forever; secrets about how to whistle through a blade of grass, how to scoop out a reed and blow a few notes through the holes, how to catch a small fish with bare hands, how to follow the track of a hare, how to read the sky.

One day they were rock climbing and Old Paul decided to try the hard way. Halfway up he got stuck while Pat looked on from below. He thought it was the end then, he confided to his trembling grandson afterwards. He could not move his hands or feet. He was petrified among the rocks. He was on the point of panic because his strength was gone. As he began to fall he was, he said, suddenly empowered; his energy blazed forth; his muscles loosened and his hands and feet moved unerringly and with a precision that was normally beyond him. 'Had I been borne aloft on wings, my deliverance could not have been more complete', he whispered to Pat that night. He had no doubt, he added, that it was his Guardian Angel. Pat was not allowed to attend the funeral. His baby sister needed minding. He knew he shouldn't cry but he raged inside at this injustice. He would have given anything to say goodbye to his best friend with the others at the graveyard. To ease his pain he wrote his essay for the following day on his friendship with his grandfather. But the substitute teacher was unaware of the pathos involved; he punished Pat for sloppy work and an unfinished sentence. Pat stopped trusting teachers then and somehow sensed that his mourning for his grandfather would never be complete.

There was another time when a chill crept into Pat's heart and never left it. It was a cold, wet, blustery February evening. Pat was in seventh heaven. In front of the open fire, surrounded by his six newly-born puppies, he was happier than he could ever remember. He picked them up one by one and rubbed them to his cheek. Their eyes were open and he could see that they liked him, and they all had different expressions. One he would call 'Sunshine', another 'Sulky', and another 'Micko'. Trixie their mother was looking on with maternal pride and total trust. Old Paul was alive then. He loved all animals but this evening his face was glowing with delight. 'God comes to life again', he used to say, 'with every new birth'.

Suddenly the door opened and Pat's father strode in. He was already angry over something but when he saw the pups in front of the fire he shouted, 'Get those bleddy mongrels out of here immediately; go drown 'em in the river'. Pat had seen that hard face before, had heard that menacing voice. It was not a time to argue. His stomach contracted with fear. There would be no reprieve. His brother had just poured some warm milk in a pan for them—their first and last meal of a brief life. His eyes already blurring with tears, Pat gently lifted and kissed each helpless handful as he placed it, with some rocks, in a sack. Their bare knees stung by the driving, wet wind, Pat and his brother, in a cortege of two, headed for the swollen river. They said nothing, but their small hearts burned with a savage hatred for the callous executioner at home having his supper. Trixie limped behind, drooping and mourning her children. Pat's ashen face was set like granite as he watched the unwilling rocks carry the bundle of new life to the bottom of the unwilling river. And his suddenly cold eyes held a warning of the silent gathering storm that would relentlessly rage around his heart at the careless and unnecessary injustice of what had just happened. Back at the house, framed in the doorway, crucified against the kitchen light, his hands raised in mute grief to the purple sky, the frail figure of his grandfather symbolised the pain of the world. More than six puppies died that evening when justice was betrayed for an innocent seven-year-old heart.

They were leaving the bog early one June evening because the mission was starting in their parish. It was Pat's first time going. He was looking forward to it so much because everyone would be there and also, he had just made his First Holy Communion so he could now receive with the grown-ups. He loved the atmosphere of the church at night—the flickering shadows from the small candles, the urgent wind outside, the reassuring hymns, and sometimes, the rich, mysterious smell of incense. They were going home through the fields, Old Paul and himself, taking a short-cut before the dark. As they climbed over a stonewall fence, Pat, in the lead, looked back to help his grandfather up. Old Paul had stopped, a look of awe on his face. Without a word he pointed to a wild flower, a fragile Oxeye Daisy, lonely and lovely, white as a cloud, perfect against the green grass and yellow moss. With his big, strong hands he cupped the petals like one might touch the face of a small baby.

Eventually, they got home, had a quick supper and made it to the church in the nick of time. The sermon frightened Pat. He did not recognise the God that Fr. Dwyer was talking about; a God who punished people severely for their mistakes, who permitted tragedies to happen all over the world, who denied unbaptised babies their heritage of heaven, who devised an eternity of agony for those who died in sin. This was not the God of the flowers that day, the lovely God of his grandfather or the playful God of his own small heart. 'Test your endurance of fire', the preacher warned, 'place your finger over a lighted candle'. Pat shivered. The people were quiet. 'Don't incur the wrath of God', he thundered, 'and don't be seduced by the false beauty of a wicked world'. The missioner was getting carried away about the devil who was lurking in their midst, seeking souls to devour. Every sin must be told in confession, every penance completed in detail. Pat was terrified now. This awful picture of a God who could only forgive and love conditionally, of a distant Ruler who did not trust the world, of an angry Judge who let you get away with nothing—all of this destroyed something beautiful in Pat's dream of the church he loved. Sadly, he placed his cold hand in the hard familiar hand of his grandfather, and he wept.

Patrick:
Paddy's True Inner Self

Patrick is the other self of Paddy. He cannot be situated historically in place and time like Paddy and Pat. He is Paddy's true, hidden voice, his real, inner self, his inmost soul. Patrick is the spirit of bonding between Pat and Paddy. He is the one who remembers the original vision of childhood, the early qualities of play, trust and delight, the natural wisdom and sense of justice that characterises the young heart. Patrick is deeply aware of the wounded child in Paddy. He is committed to the healing of early wounds so that the inner, eternal child can be embraced and befriended by Paddy. Patrick is the spirit of connecting and completing, the Celtic angel of wholeness and wholesomeness that eventually brings full identity and power to Paddy.

Put in another way, Patrick may be regarded as the child mystic in Paddy's heart, the image of God at his centre, the voice of his innate wisdom. He is aware of the contemplative soul of Pat, the lost dream of Paddy and the spiritual journey toward the reclaiming of integrity. His responsibility is the recovery of inner and outer harmony for Paddy. In short, Patrick can see the full picture. He is Paddy's guide to a new freedom, a deeper joy, a second journey toward his own truth and the abundant life promised to all those who follow their dreams with a divine passion.

What follows is a series of conversations between Patrick and Paddy on a number of topics that are central to personal growth and social transformation. At times, Patrick will be the mature voice of the inner child that heals and loves Paddy into his intended wholeness and truth; at other times, he will play the part of the Celtic wise man who guides and counsels with gentleness and authority. He may speak with the wider, universal resonance of the eternal soul that uncovers love and meaning in every experience, that sets all words to music, that flows like an underground river to water a thirsty, empty heart by nourishing it toward its appointed destiny. Finally, Patrick can be seen as the holy whisper of Love's spirit to awaken the sleeping imagination of Paddy's soul.

Patrick, then, aware of the wounded child of Paddy's youth—the child we call Pat—and aware too of the present state of stagnation and confusion in Paddy's middle years, endeavours to reconcile the frictions and fractures through which the joy, beauty and creativity have seeped from Paddy's life.

PART 2

Conversations

Conversations
Between Paddy and Patrick

Paddy, as we have seen, is reluctantly seeking help. He is not himself, feeling trapped in some invisible prison from which he longs to be set free. But how does he begin his journey to freedom? Especially when there is nobody he can talk to.

In these pages, we have also taken a brief look at Paddy's childhood, through the eyes of Pat. Graced with a beautiful, free spirit, Pat closely identifies with nature, enjoying many experiences of deep communion and ecstasy. For a better understanding of Paddy, we also took note of three occasions when the mystical spirit of the seven-year-old was crushed by incidents at home, in school and in church.

Patrick, our third *persona*, is the deepest Paddy, the voice of wisdom of the healed child whose only calling is to restore to Paddy his original blessing, his potential to be beautiful as God is beautiful. Patrick's heart beats strong and true in Pat; it no longer beats in Paddy.

The time has now come for an open dialogue between Paddy, the mid-life adult, and Patrick, his deepest being, his inner spiritual teacher. These conversations are about inner healing, a fresh start, overcoming addictions, letting go of fear, befriending pain, becoming more compassionate, and growing in trust, creativity and love.

What is central to each conversation is the role of Pat, the wounded child of wonder. It is he who holds the key that unlocks the door to freedom for Paddy. That is why he keeps cropping up in the dialogue that follows.

About Trusting

The days and weeks after his visit to the doctor brought no relief for Paddy. One night he came as near as he ever did to praying. He also came very close to desperation. Eileen had gone on her first-ever weekend retreat. Maybe it was the rare experience of being alone in the house that brought his distress to a head. Whatever the reason, late into his sleepless night, he pleaded in panic for help. Sooner than he expected, he had come to the end of the line. His silent cry came from within the prison of his long-buried feelings—a desperate plea for guidance, for peace. Love is always waiting to heal such broken spirits. Love has legions of angels who use a million disguises to touch the hurting places and so begin the road to wholeness. When Paddy was drifting in the space between sleeping and wakefulness, he had the following conversation with his inner guide, Patrick.

Patrick: I have been waiting for you to call for help. You have been hurt and very withdrawn for many years. You have trusted no one; you were brought up that way. But now you are beginning to examine your life, to reflect on your emotions, to feel again. I know it is a painful time. It all looks fairly depressing but I will go with you on the journey—a second journey into your inner spirit that will reveal surprising news about yourself.

Paddy: Will you help me to see what's happening to me and not go away? What a relief it is to admit my pain to you and to myself. How I've struggled for years with this growing unrest, blaming my job, my wife, my age. And drinking more doesn't help. Neither do more vigorous work-outs. Why do I find it so hard to open myself up to anyone? Will I ever be able to?

Patrick: Your journey is only beginning. But the first step covers half the distance. You have held so much in for so long. Your anxieties and fears began to fester when you forced them into the corners of your soul. Throw off the mask that you've been wearing for years. Start trusting your own heart, and see what happens! You will begin to feel better when you start getting in touch with your feelings. Much of your pain is coming from blocked memories and suppressed emotions.

Paddy: I hope you are right. But why do I find it so hard to trust?

Patrick: You are not alone in this. The reasons are usually found somewhere in childhood. People carry hurts from the past that influence the way they grow up—an influence that is often deeper than they suspect. The kind of personality, the quality of life, the level of joy—all are directly connected with what happens in the early years. Many carry wounds so severe that they remain crippled for a long time.

Paddy: I think I follow you. But what have these hurts to do with trusting?

Patrick: As a child, you had a natural openness and confidence in those who came into your world. You may well remember, some day soon, experiences from the past that affected you profoundly, experiences of deep disappointment or disillusionment. There may have been times when, for one reason or another, people close to you failed you. There may be moments of betrayal that you have forgotten, but which are still buried alive inside you. These are the wounds you must identify, acknowledge, and heal before trusting becomes, once again, second nature to your spirit.

Paddy: Sometimes I have vague memories of distressing moments from my childhood. Have I blotted these out of my mind to avoid further hurting? Is this connected with my inability to trust?

Patrick: Very likely. When you were a child, you trusted completely. You trusted your parents and all adults. You trusted your grandfather. But when he died, nobody tried to help you understand a little of the mystery of death and life. You were not allowed to go to his funeral or to grieve in the normal way. You felt let down then. Your trust has been betrayed many times since by adults. You slowly began to lose this special grace. You were already deciding unconsciously that you would never love or trust again. You began to freeze up. But soon you will begin to let some warmth into the cold secrets of your childhood.

Paddy: All this is new to me. It's exciting, but frightening as well. How do I start? When do I begin?

Patrick: You will know when it's right for you to travel back to your past. Maybe the time is now. It seems to me that you are ready. There are ways of allowing the suppressed feelings to emerge. You must be very careful. These memories and emotions can be quite powerful and must be truly respected. Sometimes it is very desirable, and often necessary, to seek professional help. After a while, the doors of memory will open when you trust a friend, trust meditation, trust in the love that is God. You will recall occasions of deep pain, arising from unexpected put-downs, feelings of being let down by parents, feelings of shock at the small God of the priests. So often the desires and hopes of your young heart were not honoured or cherished. You will remember the times when your teachers and parents were careless with your dreams. They misunderstood and misinterpreted your good intentions. Unknowingly, they blamed you in the wrong. All kinds of scary surprises may come up for you when you discover the path to your subconscious.

Paddy: What effect will all this have on me? It sounds very traumatic.

Patrick: It can be. It depends on how stuck you are and how deep the wounds go. One effect of recovering such memories is the experience of anger, often intense and disturbing. You realise that your potential for joy has been seriously limited, blocked by the small wall you were forced to erect around your vulnerable heart. So don't be surprised, then, if you go through a time of resentment toward certain individuals and groups of people, until you break through again into further growth.

Paddy: What kind of breakthrough are you talking about?

Patrick: As your inner self becomes increasingly healed of its early hurts, you will experience a new freedom in your life. There will be a power of trusting. First of all, you will trust yourself more—you will believe in your own heart and begin to follow its guidance. You will be able to talk to Eileen. You will also communicate more regularly and deeply with one or two carefully chosen friends, and be amazed at how good you feel afterwards. Then people who make the mid-life breakthrough often renew their trust in general—in life itself, in the future and the special place they will play in it, in the everpresent love of God. When you come through this mid-life darkness, you will always know that, if ever in the decades ahead you are in danger of going under and you reach out your hand in trust, someone will take it.

It was at this point that Paddy woke up, and shook his head in wonder. Maybe he could trust after all. Maybe someone would take his hand and lead him to his true destiny. The inner voice was so compelling! It was all so strange, but he wasn't frightened. He was beginning to believe that something very important was going on in his heart; that he was being called out of a cautious, closed attitude which had crept into his life since he came back home from England many years ago; that he would find a new excitement in living if he could only open up and let go a little more, and also that, having lost his faith in the church, he might find now a fresh and challenging trust in love.

About Mid-Life

Paddy was shocked and disgusted with himself. His hopes had been high after his dream. He was sitting in the car outside the house, having come back from the pub, with his head in his hands. What had come over him today? Why did he shout at the pupils and argue so bitterly with Seán and Mick tonight? This morning he fought with Eileen for no real reason. He had felt numb and very tense all day. The drink hadn't helped. Like the doctor said, he was hurting from inside; something deep within was causing the stress and depression, the deep-seated exhaustion and emotional unevenness, the disturbed sleep and the physical aches.

Earlier in the evening, when he had locked the school, Kay, his assistant, had casually suggested that he might like to take tomor-

row off, or go away with Eileen for a long weekend. He pretended not to hear. He didn't want anyone to notice or know how flat, empty and desperate he felt. In fact, apart from that strange dream, he had denied and hidden his pain from himself. But he could do this no longer. His father's death was the last straw. Depressed by the alcohol, and overcome by a feeling of uselessness and self-rejection, he cried aloud in the darkness and silence of the car. 'Oh help me, someone! For God's sake, help me, help me!' Suddenly, he was calm and listening....

Patrick: I am here. You're not alone. The need to call out in your pain should not alarm you. It will happen from time to time. Your desperation can be the cause of a very important step forward in your life. You have suffered enough in silence. But all of this is a blessing in disguise even though you may not see it that way now. There is no growing without pain and this is the moment of a new beginning, a turning point you will never forget. Most men in mid-life go through something like this. It is a predictable crisis but not necessarily a predictable transition. Many get stuck. Tell me more about your feelings right now.

Paddy: I'm feeling now what I've been feeling for years. But I never told anyone. Who would understand? How was I to know that this crisis was a common occurrence? Mick and Seán did not talk about it. Maybe men don't. More's the pity I suppose.

Anyway, I have a sinking feeling of losing control over my life, a feeling of uncertainty about everything. I'm not sure about the meaning of life—I never even thought about it before. It all seems so pointless, all the effort, all the pressure, all the crap you must take from people. I feel like a victim now, pestered by my staff, the students and their parents, even my own family. There are different ways of putting it. What a relief to talk about it! I feel restless and trapped. I feel disillusioned with the whole thing. And the church is no use to me anymore. A few years ago it was different. There was the excitement of the family growing up, enjoying their successes, planning their future with Eileen. My job was interesting, I was promoted, I was good at it. I added extensions to the house, grew our own vegetables, coached the school basketball team. But it's all over. There's nothing to look forward to now except the TV and the pub. I feel desperate. In fact, a few times I could have gone and done it—you know what I mean! It was that bad last Christmas. And still I told no one.

Patrick: There is a profound re-shaping going on within you. Your self-image is very low because you have not yet discovered your new priorities, new values, new goals. Your original vision of childhood has not yet been fulfilled. This time around it will be. The job, the sports, the buddies, the pub—all of these are important in your life. But now you are ready to move on. You feel strain and tension because the beliefs and ambitions of the past do not sustain you anymore. You have a sense of loss about that, and anger too. In time you will learn how to grieve for the passing of that season of your life, even as you gain a new perspective on the meaning of living, a perspective that is challenging and exciting.

Paddy: I think you understand how I feel, but I do not share your optimism about my condition.

Patrick: Well, you do have a journey before you. The journey is not backwards. It is onward and outward. And it need not be long and hard. Much of it is about letting go rather than doing violence to yourself with fierce, white-knuckle will-power. Gently you will regain control of your life. At the moment you have lost it. That is why your self-

respect is so low. Your inner resources are severely under-
nourished. You have lost touch with your centre. You are
off-balance. Once you begin to experience the healing, the
flow of a returning emotional health, then a new joy in living each day will flood your soul.

Paddy: You're great with the words, lad. But why don't you
tell me *how* to make this transition into a finer quality of
life?

Patrick: No one can tell you that. Only your own heart can.
And it will. But you must learn how to listen to it. I can
make some suggestions about how to begin. They are well-
known but not well-embraced.

Because of the remarkable intimacy between our emotional state and our physical condition, there is a constant
interaction within us. An abused body will immediately
cause distress of spirit. On the other hand, three fourths of
all bodily illness are stress-related. Regular, appropriately
energetic exercise for half an hour, five days a week, is already the beginning of a lasting recovery. A frantic, guilty
squash court workout on the evening of a hangover does
not come under the heading of regular exercise. Excessive
drinking is an insidious practice. It intensifies the anxiety it
promises to relieve, and it makes more shallow the sleep it
promises to deepen. It is poison to the spirit.

Paddy: Don't preach at me, please! I've quit smoking. I'm
watching the booze. I'll start walking. What else? Life is
fairly empty now. There's not much left, it seems to me.

Patrick: People today are swiftly discovering a new meaning for leisure time—not as time spent in the pub, watching
TV, or in over-energetic workouts, but as a re-creation or relaxation time. This may be prime time spent with a friend,

where mutual trust is high and the sharing is deep. There is effective therapy going on when the week's suppressed feelings are expressed, often forcefully, in the sacred space offered by a soul-friend, when secrets are shared and doubts revealed. Underlying emotions are recalled, named, owned and expressed. Only then can they be let go of. Soul-friends know how to listen. It is the necessary gift that makes the relief and growing possible. We are not afraid that we will be rejected when we tell people who we really are. Tomorrow, they will tell us who they are.

Paddy: What is a soul-friend? How do I find one?

Patrick: In early Celtic spirituality, the monks were strongly urged to acquire or accept an *anamchara*, a soul-friend, to support and guide them on their spiritual journey. The *anamchara* did this by being a good listener and a trusted counsellor. The same is recommended for us today. It is so important to be able to let off stream to someone on a regular basis, but also to talk about our deepest concerns. We normally discuss everything except the most important issues in our lives—our hopes and our fears, our aspirations and our doubts, the true health of our hearts and of our souls. Pals they may well be, but I don't see Mick and Séan as the soul-friends you need at this moment in your life.

Where can you find one? You can't. He or she will find you. There's an old Buddhist saying, 'When you are ready, the teacher will come'. In your leisure time you may explore the possibility of pursuing some creative hobbies. Think of some interest you have, or had, but never got round to pursuing. It could be woodwork or pottery, writing or painting, learning a language or a musical skill, cultivating your own garden again. The actual participation in these creative activities begins to heal us by reaching into our feelings and expressing them imaginatively in an artistic manner. The chances of finding a soul-friend there are higher, I suspect, than in a pub. But then, who knows?

Paddy: No need to get derisive. Let me tell you some of the questions I keep asking myself these days. I wonder why everything is a drag, why nothing is done out of conviction or passion, only out of duty. And I always feel dumped on by everybody. Why can't I say 'no' occasionally? I'm afraid of being criticised; I'm always looking for approval and praise. Why do I neglect Eileen, never taking time out to do any of the activities you just mentioned, either alone or with her? Why am I afraid to take a stand on issues that are important to me, always settling for peace at any price? There are many more questions. It all seems rather hopeless.

Patrick: The very fact of describing these anxieties just now will bring its own relief later. That, in itself, is a source of renewed energy. So is everything that helps us to know ourselves better. Honest, affirming communication is hard to beat. Also, reflecting on, or discussing, your dreams can be exceptionally revealing, but, I suggest for the time being, not in the pub with Mick and Seán.

In the meantime, examine any one of your list of questions. Why are you victimised for instance? But you're not—at least no more than anybody else. What's happening is that you are victimising yourself. Nobody can burden you without your permission. It's not what somebody says to you that lowers your self-esteem; it's what you say to yourself when the other person stops talking. So avoid distorting your experiences; otherwise you will develop a persecution complex, keep blaming yourself, and stay stuck. For example, don't overgeneralise and complain, 'This *always* happens to me'. Don't focus on the negative comments out of many positive affirmations, e.g., allowing one negative remark to negate a dozen positive ones.

You sound as though you jump to conclusions too; just because one disturbed pupil is restless you probably assume the whole class is bored. Do you also take responsibility for others by, for instance, blaming yourself if a parent complains about a teacher on your staff? It is quite surprising how quickly we reclaim our power in every way, once we succeed in reclaiming it in any way; how we assume control over our whole lives once we do it first in any one area. But we cannot hold anything back; all the shady areas must be exposed fearlessly to the light. You will need special support to begin.

Paddy: And this is what also worries me—I *have* no support. In fact, believe it or not, I'm lonely. I'm a lonely man. I don't feel loved. I don't even feel important. I don't seem to have value any more. I never thought it would all turn out like this. If my present perception is true, then I must have been living in a fantasy world up to a few years ago.

Patrick: You have been. But like everyone else, you must now accept the unreality of your fantasies and live in the world as it is, not as you dream it to be. This adjustment is very painful for some. You are facing the pain, you are befriending this loneliness. It is so important for you to reflect deeply on the unfolding mystery of your growth. The death of a father is a very significant moment in a son's life. It is traumatic because he now has to face his own mortality in a new and shocking way. This is a scary and very lonely time—the time you are in now.

You are lonely, too, because Eileen is growing and assuming an independence you don't quite understand. And this frightens you. She has done an excellent job of raising the children, and is now letting them go. It is a type of death for her. But her own spiritual and emotional growth are of vital importance to her. She is free now to develop her artistic talents and enjoy a kind of freedom that many men enjoy but which is denied to women until their children leave home.

So of course you're lonely. The family has grown up and you are only now beginning to realise it. You must adjust to that. Your job, at the moment, is isolating. Can you think of ways to open it up and out into the community, bringing your staff with you, finding creative and exciting ways to enrich the quality of people's lives?

Like all the aspects of the mid-life transition, loneliness has a *spiritual* dimension. This is something that men tend to forget, but it holds the key to the healing and growing that will liberate them from their isolation and confusion.

As Paddy unlocked the front door, a falling leaf danced around him in the glow of the streetlight. This autumn he was noticing with a new awareness the fall of the leaf from the tree. There was a split second when, ever so gently, each leaf lets go, at its vital stem, of the only contact with its source of life on the branch. What an awful, ordinary moment! So too with all of us, thought Paddy, as intimations of his own mortality echoed in his soul. But tonight he noticed too the new dancing of the finally liberated leaf. It seemed to be lightly playing a deadly serious game of immortality—like all dancers do who, quick on their feet, refuse to acknowledge the downward pull of the gravity of death, holding themselves in perfect balance between heaven and earth. A Kerry phrase of hope brought a smile to his tired face. He liked the hint of wildness in the concept of heaven as the síamsa Dé, the divine fiesta led by the Lord of the Dance himself.

About Healing

Every now and then Paddy would pause to examine one of the photographs. He was looking through old albums for a decent snapshot of his father to put in the mortuary card. The house was quiet. Eileen was at her gardening class. Paddy was thinking about his Dad. Because he never really knew him, he hadn't felt much loss at the funeral a few weeks earlier. He felt guilty about their poor relationship, about visiting him only out of duty, about showing false concern.

A photograph drifted to the floor—an old brown school snapshot of himself taken when he was seven or eight. Slightly freckled, excited and wide-eyed, a shy grin, proud of a smart checked jacket sent from his aunt in New York. Visible behind the big knot in his tie, holding the collars of his new-looking shirt together, was a gold tie-pin. Plastered with Brylcreem, his hair was straight, flat and greasy. Without warning, and straight from the pit of his guts, came a sound, the likes of which Paddy had never made before. It was a sound of anguish and pain. It seemed to carry within it the anger of years, the cry of ages. This explosion of rage settled into long, moaning sobs that shook his stocky frame for some time. He noticed that his tears were falling on the faded photograph he was still holding. The delighted dreamy face was communicating courage to him. From deep within, his spirit spoke....

Patrick: Go ahead, Paddy, and cry; you are holding those tears for a long time, too long. So don't be shocked by this. Something very important is happening. A huge, buried block of suppressed emotion is lifting. This is the beginning of your breakthrough. Keep crying. Dead, festering remains of abuse and rejection, especially from your childhood time, are being swept away. Imagine carrying that stuff around with you for the rest of your life! No wonder you were stuck.

Paddy: This has never happened before. It's quite frightening. Are you sure I'm not cracking up?

Patrick: Of course you're not. Crying is nature's way of

relieving pressure and healing hurts. You might have been
in deep trouble if this had not happened. The world is full
of people who are haunted by past guilt, weighed down by
a wakening sense of their own inadequacy. For some, the
healing is quick and traumatic; for others it happens over a
longer period. In your case it is twofold. After this fairly
sudden breakthrough, you must make sure that the healing
continues at all costs.

Paddy: Why are you so sure that this is good for me?

Patrick: You are doing so well! Already there is a change.
But it takes time. There is no shortcut to emotional and
mental health. When we deny our emotions at any stage of
our lives, the pain goes underground. Deeply buried pain is
highly destructive. We bury it by ignoring it, denying it and
avoiding it. It is impossible to pursue this kind of violence
to the spirit and to the body without serious emotional inju-
ry. Most neuroses, we're told, are caused by the avoidance
of necessary pain. Your build-up of imprisoned feelings
burst out tonight because you were ready, even though you
did not consciously know that. But now you do.

So, try to find someone you can trust completely. That
person will help you to discover the sources of your hurt
from the past. That person—your soul-friend, the *anamcha-*
ra—will help you to cry, to get angry, to use colourful language, to shout. We all need a good listener to trust because
we can only know and love as much of ourselves as we are
willing to share with and release to another.

Paddy: What do you think sparked off my little breakdown
just now?

Patrick: It was not a breaking down, but a 'healing up'.
Your emotional system could take no more pretense;

neither could your tense, nervous body. Something had to
happen, and lucky for you it did! The final push came from
the combined emotional impact of your father's funeral and
the photo in your hand.

Let me explain how I see it. It goes back a long way and
is really quite complicated at the beginning. Tell me if I'm
making any sense. When you were small and vulnerable,
you adored your grandfather. You were very distressed
when your Dad left you at home on the day of the funeral.
Your mourning was never completed. That need is still
there. Every funeral you have attended since then has stim-
ulated those memories, maybe subconsciously, and kept the
need and the wound open. Your father's funeral was a powerful reminder of your unfinished grieving. It also brought
home to you, without your conscious awareness of it, the
unexpressed resentment you still hold for your father because of what happened that day. Does any of this strike a
chord with you?

Paddy: You seem to be reaching back into the mists of my
past. It is very strange. My head says you're talking through
your hat, but my heart knows you're right. Even as we reflect together, I'm becoming aware of the feelings I had
when I was shouting and crying just now. I *do* have a burning anger inside me. I suddenly have a picture of putting
rocks in a sack to drown some lovely pups on a harsh, empty Sunday evening around the time of my First Communion. Oh yes, I remember it now. 'I'll kill that bastard', I
whispered to a heartbroken Trixie as her squealing puppies
were carried off in the brown flood. Look, I'm shaking; the
rage, the pain, the hurt are still so strong within me. Will
they damage me? What can I do to handle them?

Patrick: They will heal you. When you face your pain, befriend and express it, your healing begins. So many of us try

to avoid our inside pain by all kinds of distractions—over-working, over-eating, hours of TV watching each day, as well as the usual list of addictions. Drinking, punishing work-outs, and constant ridiculing of others will not heal us. They drain us of our power, our creativity and our daily joy. Just look around you at your peers and colleagues; look beneath the surface. Can you see how they are stuck?

Sometimes it takes a shock of some kind to wake up a heart; to spark the realisation that one is living in a box of fear or guilt or anger; to discover that, from childhood on, we have been trying to live up to someone else's expectations, to please others. It is only after a near-fatal accident, a heart attack, the admission that one is an alcoholic, a death in the family, or some form of mid-life crisis that many people find another way of living, a more positive, praising, trusting, 'aware' kind of presence to everyone and everything. People who are making this type of journey will tell you about how free they feel, how awake they are to the miracles going on around them, how much energy they are finding to be creative in all kinds of ways.

Paddy: How can a crisis make me feel free?

Patrick: Sometimes a crisis forces us to examine our lives more deeply. Mourning is one of the ways of being healed, of being set free from sadness and loss. But it is a way we often neglect or avoid. I believe that it is very important for our well-being to mourn every day. Have you noticed the flicker of sorrow in people's faces, the grief in the shape of the body, the unbidden tears that spring up into the eyes? There is a lurking sadness inside us that needs to be expressed—a sadness that has to do with the necessary losses in our lives, such as youth, health, fulfillment, success. We mourn for the unfulfilled expectations we had of ourselves—our potential, our dreams, our visions. We mourn for our high hopes of career success, of marriage, of ministry. We mourn for lost loves, broken promises, and repeated failures. And so we need to pause and mourn. If we dare to love, we must be prepared to grieve. We cannot grow, we cannot have or spread joy, if there is no outlet for our daily grief, in tears or talk or some kind of external ritual.

Paddy: What do you mean by ritual?

Patrick: Let me mention a very public and intense one. The normal funeral service is a very powerful moment—maybe even more so in the days of the violet vestments and the haunting, evocative 'De profundis'. Public mourning is very nesessary at certain times. Effective bereavement often requires the expression of grief in front of others. That is what you missed when your grandfather was buried: the consolation from others, the ritual of walking to the grave, seeing the coffin lowered into the earth, hearing the prayers and the weeeping of the people in the cemetery. It is one of the few occasions when men have permission to cry in public. But you didn't even feel free to cry alone. That time was really hard for you. Your grandad was the one you loved more than anybody else. You were very confused and hurt. And they never talked to you about his death or gave you a chance to grieve for him. I think your father's death might be bringing back now the pain that you could not express then. But take it gently. You cannot force the river. It will all unfold as it should. Trust deeply.

Paddy: Well, I'll surely need to trust deeply to forgive them for all that!

Patrick: Real forgiveness is always about healing. When we forgive someone, both ourselves and the other person are healed. Especially ourselves. The hard heart affects our bodily and mental health. It is ourselves we let off the hook when we forgive. We cannot grow when we withhold forgiveness. Especially if we withhold it from ourselves. I believe that a great number of people dislike or hate themselves, because they were given a very low opinion of themselves when small, because they were heavily criticised at home and maybe in school, because they were loved very conditionally. They now suffer from low self-esteem and often even self-hate. That is why self-forgiveness can be so difficult, especially for those who project the conditional forgiveness of their parents on to God. For such people, the wounded child must be healed back where the hurting appeared.

Paddy: You've talked about forgiveness and healing, but is there anything else that would help to heal the wounded child?

Patrick: Whatever stimulates our creativity, brings the artist within us to life, arouses our fascination, helps us to contemplate, awakens the sleeping mystic within us; whatever succeeds in achieving this heals us deeply at the centre. It is in our vitality and creativity that we truly resemble God. We co-create with love. God needs us to incarnate divine beauty on this earth. Not only do we become healed, we also become God-like when those divine powers are released within us.

That is why creative hobbies are therapeutic. So many people are attending adult education classes and courses and workshops on spiritual growth, and are rediscovering their creativity by learning about counselling skills and imaginative meditation techniques. Many who had never attempted to dance, draw, write, paint, work with clay, massage, or play music, because of put-downs when they were small, are now taking heart again and finding exciting resources for inspiration, relaxation and meditation within their own spirits. In some way or another, Eileen and Peggy are aware of all this. They are calling to the child-teacher within to come out to play; to teach them to dance again, to let go, to be happy.

And remember, tonight has seen your first great step. You are on your way. Don't be fretting about the time ahead. Your heart will guide you. Trust it.

By the time Eileen returned, he had cleaned up the schoolboy snapshot and placed it in a small picture-frame, which had long stood empty, on his personal bookshelf over the fire. Above it, with its heavy tick-tock, stood the revered family time-piece. It was a good place to keep in touch with his child—under the eye of the clock.

About Growing

Paddy was horrified at what he was thinking. Because he was reviewing his life these days, his fondness for alcohol was becoming obvious to him. He had often tried to cut down; he would also increase his time on the squash court after heavy binges, and most years he went off drink for Lent. He knew that while drinking had become central to his life, and that he may well have a problem with it, he was definitely not an alcoholic. But could he be sure? This was the awful possibility dawning on him. Equally shocking was his next thought—should he give it up? He was awake early with these startling thoughts. As he waited for the alarm clock to divide the night from the day, he tossed and turned and worried. Why was he changing—giving up so much? What would be left? Once again, the familiar comforting voice brought relief.

Patrick: Remember, Paddy, that you are in your forties, a time of many choices. At a certain age, often around midlife, some people become aware of a desire to clean up their lives, to ask themselves what is really important as the decades fly by. They find that the business of living—professional competition, marriage concerns, social expectations, financial anxieties—has taken a heavy toll on their emotional and spiritual growth. You are beginning to know what I mean. You, too, are suffering from a famine of the heart, a hunger of the spirit. The original vision of your childhood has been lost along the way. This happens to most people. They compromise, they settle for less, they lose integrity in their own eyes and in the eyes of others. The deeper needs are not met anymore. So much can go wrong with the delicate balance of souls when they are untrue to their unique nature. All are spiritual creatures with an unquenchable desire for intimacy with beauty, with love, with what they call God. So often, however, people try to satisfy that desire with more immediate satisfaction; they slake their thirst at clouded wells, and rely for their inspiration on flawed sources.

Paddy: Are you saying we don't know who we really are?

Patrick: You have forgotten that you are a creature of splendour and glory. You have great difficulty in taking your divine origin seriously. It is extraordinary how low the self-image of so many is, how disempowered they are through a fear picked up in childhood. People's true selves are hidden. They are never ankle-deep in who they really are. They engage but a fraction of their transforming, healing power. But you are waking up. You are getting in touch with your true self, your feelings, your brokenness and your power. You are ready.

Paddy: How do I begin the journey? And how do I keep travelling? It's all very different from my normal way of thinking.

Patrick: The fact that you have asked the question shows that you have already begun. Just call on the power of the universe, the creator of life; call on the love that is invincible and that is crazy about you in particular, and changes will begin to happen. The impossible becomes possible. Like the radio or the bulb that is dead until it is plugged in and then comes to life with music and light, so too will you come to life. Talk to the infinite power and love in whose image you are meticulously designed, and through whose divine spirit you can change and grow. Simply trust. You will be transfigured and transformed. Your mind will fill with exciting thoughts, your body will dance with health, and your heart will sing with freedom.

Paddy: Sounds too good to be true—for me anyway. I don't know when or where to begin.

Patrick: You are ready. Start anywhere. Look at your addictions. Go for the big one. Don't get overly anxious about the journey. Just let it happen. You will grow, not by willpower but by soul-power; not by daily determination but by going with the flow of the eternal river of life. Let love take over. There is nothing impossible for you now. There are no limits. You have listened to the inner call from the wise and wounded child who will heal you. Follow that call. It will lead you to another way of living, to another countryside of the spirit which you will recognise as your longed-for homeland. Every cell in your body, every life-force on earth, every season and every dream, all are on your side. And speak to the angels, who carry you unerringly toward the light when the mist is heavy.

Paddy: I'm with you in spots. And I desperately want to grow and to trust. But why do I find it so hard to let go? I clutch at things.

Patrick: There is something in us that wants to cling to people and things. This may stem from fear and insecurity. There is a compulsion in us to own, to have power over, to control, to manipulate.

The clinging may arise from our misplaced searching for fulfillment, beauty and love. We take the wrong road. We miss the turn. We don't identify what really satisfies us in a lasting way. In our short pleasures and long addictions we settle for small gods.

Another reason for holding on is our drive to possess what we are attracted toward—ideas, material things, people. Because we are in God's image, we desire God; we desire all that is lovely, free, open and ecstatic. That is the attraction that draws us, the motivation that empowers us. But possessiveness has no part in our divine desire. The possessive heart is radically destructive; it destroys the object of its desire. To achieve the freedom we are talking about, to follow the dream that haunts us, to answer the call of the carefree child within us, we must let go of clinging, of possessiveness. There is no other way to gain peace of mind, to avoid getting stuck. We can only let go when we trust. Letting go is something we must be doing all the time. It is so easy to get hooked on almost anything. Eventually letting go becomes second nature to us, as comfortable as breathing. But that takes a very long time.

Paddy: All this too sounds a bit new. Is 'letting go' like giving something away or doing without something or surrendering?

Patrick: It is all these things. We do it to grow. It sounds like a contradiction but we grow by letting go. We grow by subtraction, someone said. We can only keep forever what we give away in love. In fact, we only truly own what we let go. There is a sense in which whatever we give away, we give away to ourselves. Whatever is given up under the impulse of love becomes the most loving part of ourselves. There is no loss which cannot lead to gain. It is true to say that we can only know and love as much of ourselves as we are willing to share or give away to another. Sometimes we must let go of certain teachings and knowledge if we are to grow in wisdom. We may even have to let go of our present image of God if we are to grow into a more mysterious and loving one.

Paddy: Would it follow, then, that in letting go of grudges and prejudices, in forgiving others, I'm really forgiving myself and at the same time enjoying God's forgiveness?

Patrick: That's a good way of putting it. But there's one more aspect of letting go. When you succeed in surrendering to the loving power all your memories of past hurts, all your remorse over yesterday's mistakes, all your regrets over what might have been, your anxieties about the future and your fears for a fragile earth, then you begin *to live in the present.* This is a most exciting and liberating moment. The present instant is the channel of God's joy; it is the only place to be if we are to experience the promised life of abundance. The *now* is always safe and healing, always comforting and hopeful. It is only through living in the now that we can become fully aware of the beauty within us, in our bodies and minds, and outside us, in other people, in the epiphanies of nature, in the mysterious universe.

Paddy: You're getting carried away again. But some of what you say makes sense.

Eileen stirred, the alarm went off. The phone and the doorbell rang together. From deep reflection to high action in five seconds.

About Praying

Paddy has taken to 'power walking'. With a pace that lies halfway between brisk striding and slow-jogging, it was widely recommended. Easy on the knees, it brought the whole body into play, involving long, springy strides. At each step the leg is stretched and the foot rolls from the heel to the toe while the arms swing deliberately and vigorously. Anyway, Paddy was power walking one evening after a parent-teacher meeting in the school. It was late autumn and there was rain in the wind. As he turned for home he heard voices singing and realised it came from the church which he was just passing. Without making a conscious effort, he found himself inside. It was Benediction. He felt the warmth. The incense was heavy in the air with its rich, sweet smell. Straight smokey wisps ascended thinly from the clusters of candles on the altar. The people were singing 'O Sacrament Most Holy' with deep reverence. Enfolded in a golden cope, the priest swung round, holding high a glittering monstrance of blessing. It was many a long year since Paddy was at Benediction. The impact on his senses released some more imprisoned recollections of childhood. The Dublin adult and the Kerry boy were once again in deep communion. It was at this emotional moment that the healing voice came quietly through.

Patrick: You probably miss those memories of your young days. But they are part of you and they are good for you, these familiar expressions of people's feelings about God and about their hopes and fears.

Paddy: I wonder why I gave it all up. Something must have gone wrong very early on.

Patrick: Let us explore a little. Do you remember when you were small you were so delighted with candles and cribs, with processions and flowers, with novenas and making the stations of the cross? And how you were thrilled during mission time in the parish, because you loved the rows of statues and pictures, the boxes of medals and trinkets in the stalls and little huts that followed the mission around the country. You liked the missioners too. But one year you seemed to change. Something must have happened. You...

Paddy: Wait. This is important. There's a buried memory inside me—a memory of pain and loss. The loss of faith. Yes. It's coming back to me. Grandad and I went to the evening session of a mission. It was just after something special had happened to us coming home through the fields. I was feeling so close to God, and the priest—I forget his name, but I remember how I hated him later—spoke about a hard God who punished people in this life and in the next, who kept unbaptised babies out of heaven and who only forgave us if we went to confession. It is all coming back to me now. How sad it is and how angry I feel! What a loss! I lost my trust in religion, I lost my love for the God of my grandad. I feel like crying now....

Patrick: Don't try to stop what's happening. Have a good cry. Hurting can be healed. It is very important that you continue to feel all these emotions. The effect of Benediction on your imagination is the grace that unlocked the cellar of your suppressed and festering memories. You may need a little help to keep up the flow that will soon bring deep peace and set you free in ways you never suspected. How are you feeling?

Paddy: Drained and empty. But I do believe that this is an essential moment in my second journey to full and satisfying living. I also believe that I must begin to pray and meditate if I'm going to keep my heart healthy and aware of beauty. Why is praying so difficult?

Patrick: It doesn't have to be. There's more to praying than saying prayers. Meditation is popular now. It can be simple and satisfying, but it is always necessary. As food is to the body, so meditation is to the spirit. It happens when we reflect deeply about the meaning of things. All our special conversations, for instance, have been one long prayer. You mentioned awareness. To be aware of the joy and pain all around is already to be meditating. Awareness is a great grace. To be totally present, to be attentive yet relaxed; to accept people in a non-judgmental way—all of these have to do with prayer, but they require a careful discipline of the spirit.

In meditation, we allow ourselves to sink deep down through all our distractions until we join the flow of God's love and are carried along by it. This is a letting go into a still point within us where there are no boundaries or limitations. It is not always an easy place to go.

Through the practice of meditation, the senses are sharpened. You heighten your power of noticing hidden colours and unusual shapes, faint sounds and different textures, the various smells in a house or field, expressions on people's faces, their postures and quality of voice. We meet the God of surprises in all of these experiences of beauty and the God of healing in the times of pain. While meditating, you could pray like this: 'I don't ask you to love me, Lord; just let me be aware of your love'.

Paddy: You seem to associate beauty a lot with prayer.

Patrick: We are born for beauty. We are naturally attracted to it, as when a child reaches for the moon, when people feel drawn to each other, or when someone follows a dream. There is hunger in us for absolute beauty, an ache for a form and a vision that elude us. We need beauty in our lives; it unlocks our deepest spirit. It is from our beauty that our finest moments come—moments of great music and art, poetry, love and vision. All beauty is the revelation of God. Our prayer enables us to remember that. It is God we are after when we pursue beauty. But we often stop searching too soon and settle for less. When we persist in the quest for beauty, however, and surround ourselves with it, we become beautiful. When we meditate on God's beauty, revealed in all creation, we are gradually transformed into the likeness of God. You might like to say this prayer, 'I don't ask you Lord for success; I ask you for beauty'.

Paddy: Sometimes you make it all sound so easy, but I find it hard. For instance, trusting in God's unconditional love and letting go of our addictions and fears. We don't really do these things very often. It seems to involve a kind of dying, a giving-away of oneself to others. Am I right?

Patrick: We can only trust when we know that we are loved. Love cannot distrust. We find it hard because we don't believe we're loved. This goes back to our wounded childhood where love so often was conditional on our behaviour. Yet our hearts are made to trust because otherwise we could not grow. When we are afraid, we stay stuck. The courage to risk is created by trust. It is risky to let go of many fears about our security, our popularity, our virtue and of many tendencies to judge, to be suspicious and to feel guilty. Letting go is the other side of trusting. So try to meditate about God taking the ultimate risk in trusting by becoming a vulnerable baby in a hostile place. In becoming human he gave himself away. In our prayer we realise that the continuation of incarnation depends on us. It is only to the extent that we are given-away people that God continues to be given-away to the world. It is at this point that we have difficulty with the evergreen Christian paradox about becoming joyful, dynamic people only when we are given-away; about having all the riches we need only when we let everything go.

Paddy: My problem with letting go are the regrets I feel about my past and fears about my future.

Patrick: That is why you so rarely live in the present. This is the way to live peacefully and effectively. Otherwise you waste so much energy in useless anxiety. Living in the present, the *now*, is always healing, always realistic. Letting go of troubled thinking brings us to our senses, to an awareness of harmony among creatures, and to an appreciation of the natural environment, animals or people in our midst. It is only in the present that God's beauty can be experienced, that the sacred and the secular meet and dance. Our meditation helps us to be still in the present; to perceive the miracles around us; to hear the silent music of continuous creation; to let go into a deep peace. In the present, you don't have to *do* anything; you simply let go and let God love you. That love, in turn, will empower you to love and liberate others.

Paddy: You make it all sound so simple. Yet in practice it is complicated. Can you explain that?

Patrick: Meditating is basically simple. It is about being quiet. It is about removing our masks of projection, of pride and prejudice. Our capacity for self-deception is inexhaustible. The wounded child must be healed. The aim is to return to a basic simplicity of vision. This is achieved by stripping away the many layers of questionable information loaded on to us when we were little. As we strip away these layers, we acquire a new sensitivity to everything around us. The simplicity we learn in silence empowers us to look and listen with our hearts. This entails much loving, and trusting, and self-forgetfulness. During such heightened awareness, God is revealed in every situation. It is an extraordinary way of being present to the world. We experience God's beauty in every beauty, God's pain in every pain. With this simplicity, the ordinary is perceived as extraordinary. A breeze, a tear, a dream, even manure—each becomes another window of wonder on God. Poets have this vision; they are able to see the face behind the face, the heart within the heart.

When we are non-judgmental, setting aside our own agenda for a while and calling on the Spirit with the trust and openness of a child, we will notice our hearts begin to flood with love. Put simply, we allow God to be God in us. We let go of our own preoccupations so that God's love can fill our hearts.

About Beauty

A week later, Paddy was sitting on a rock overlooking the sea. It was a Saturday morning and he had skipped his visit to the off-track betting office. He was in a thoughtful mood. The small, scudding clouds raced inland under a thin sun, sending circles of shadows sliding onto the shore off the flat water. The shadows moved swiftly up the hill to where he was sitting, briefly enfolding him and the rock in a deep-green moment of darkness. Paddy felt himself slipping slowly backward in time to a reverie of lost beauty. And his heart began to sing again softly to the sea, as it did on a Kerry beach many years before. He became quietly aware of a presence by his side.

Patrick: Listen carefully. Can you hear the music in the water again? Like before? It never stopped playing, you know; *you* stopped hearing it. You will soon discover why this happened, why you gradually went deaf to the music. You must learn again to listen with your heart. The tunes are playing everywhere, the beauty is all around you. You hunger for beauty; you are nourished by it. It comes in many forms. You searched for it as a child and you often found it. It is your nature to be forever drawn toward all that is beautiful because God is beauty and you are made in God's image.

Paddy: Where do I go to find the beauty of which you speak?

Patrick: Nowhere. The place of beauty is within you. It springs from the way you see the ordinary events of life. Think back to the times you sat by the sea or listened to the streams. Do you remember walking barefoot in the first warm days of spring, and the lovely feeling of sand and water against your skin? It takes a certain kind of silence for this to happen. It is only when our hearts are quiet that we can recall the music and beauty in the past, and perceive the wonder in everyday sounds and sights—a footstep on the stairs, a shadow on the floor, the grasp of a child's hand, the crunch of a wheel on gravel, the landing of a bird.

Paddy: What about pain? This is an everyday experience too. Where is the beauty there?

Patrick: Is not winter beautiful? Or the dark of night? How would Eileen talk about the pain of giving birth? What about the suffering that inspired the great works of art—the music that has recreated the hearts of millions, the paintings and poems that forever lift the spirit of humanity? Your question is about mystery. Can you have mountains without valleys, a dawn without darkness, forgiveness without hurt, love without grief? All of life is a mixture of brokenness and healing, pain and beauty.

Paddy: With pain I am familiar. But the beauty has gone.

Whatever happened to the magic of those early years, to the music of childhood?

Patrick: The joy is still there—waiting. But you have become distracted; you have drifted to sleep. You are now waking up to a new morning. You have a faithful friend, your heart, which is reminding you of your beauty, urging you to pursue your true destiny.

Paddy: Is it safe to listen to my heart?

Patrick: Your heart is always true to you. It tells no lies. To live by your heart, to walk beautifully upon the earth is the reason we were born. But first of all you must really *want* to be transformed. The cynics who ridicule or deny the original vision of childhood, the divine destiny of truth and beauty, will never see far into the mystery of life. They will never experience the deep joy of each day, the ecstasy of the ordinary, the passion for the possible. You, however, at last, are opening yourself to love; you are trusting your heart and your God; you are letting go of your anxieties and fears.

Paddy: Even though I desperately need help, why am I so slow to believe you? Why am I reluctant to commit myself to this quest for freedom and beauty? What guarantees do I have for success if I go for a breakthrough?

Patrick: Do not be anxious. You will see as we go along. But you are right. There is a peculiar resistance to growing into deeper love, to accepting beauty, to seeing the loneliness of ourselves and of all creation. This resistance is especially strong in men. I think it may be linked to a fear of developing their more gentle, compassionate sides. It is very common. You are no exception.

You also ask for certainty about the future. There is none.

Let yourself trust in love. It's as simple as that. Just stop trying to control tomorrow, to manipulate God. It is necessary
to believe that all of life—every aspect of nature, every beat
of your heart, every dream of your soul, every creature that
exists—all are pressing to empower you, to love you into
your beauty. Simply trust that there is no place for fear, anxiety or stress in this new scheme of things. You are held
close by the Mother of Love because you are her special
child. In fact you are held very close because you are extraordinarily special.

Paddy: Why wasn't I told about all this before? Where do I
find the wisdom I need to begin my second journey?

Patrick: When you were a boy you knew everything you
needed to know. You listened to your heart and it was a
perfect counsellor. It still is. Just listen to it, as you're listening now. It possesses all truth and all wisdom. It is, above
all, a thing of infinite beauty. But somewhere along the way
this heart of yours, this vision of an inner kingdom, this
dream of a universe of mercy and justice, got damaged, because people did or said harmful things to you. They destroyed your beauty. They made you feel that you were no
longer a child of wonder and loveliness. The world, as a
tour through a hospital suggests, is full of people who hate
themselves because of a wounded childhood. There is a vicious kind of negative criticism which makes young and old
think they are ugly, unclean, useless. Most adults are
wounded in that way. You certainly are, but your wounded, inner child is healing. I know. I am that light and compassion that will help to bring you and your inner child,
this lost self, together in peace and power.

Paddy: Is there not a danger in telling people that they are
beautiful? It could give them ideas, you know, especially

children. And how do you know that you are right? For instance, I never heard a sermon about beauty.

Patrick: It never hurts to let people know that they are beautiful; it brings out the best in them. We are all so slow to praise, but praise and affirmation are great healers.

All of us are images of God's eternal love. We are daughters and sons of infinite beauty. We are God's work of art. Our hearts and bodies are temples of divine love. All we have to do is to claim our beauty, become aware of our awesome power, let God dream the divine dream within us, live without limits....

Paddy: Hang on, hang on a minute. 'Live without limits'. That's a bit much, isn't it?

Patrick: We can do and become whatever we want by simply moving into the flow of the great underground river called God. The one condition to our freedom to create beauty and to heal is to remain open to the flood of blessings that empower us. The days of the church's suspicion about the value of humanity and of all creation will soon be over. Today we celebrate our original blessing.

How much do we really have to teach children about being holy, wise, and forgiving? Perhaps we should be learning from them about their innate sense of justice, wisdom and forgiveness. Whenever we honour a child's beauty we honour both God and ourselves. The same is true of the smallest creature. Once a Zen master stood up before his students to deliver a sermon on beauty. And just as he was about to open his mouth a bird sang. 'The sermon', he said, 'has been delivered'.

Before Paddy could raise the question about the destructive side of young people, a fresh breeze sprang up bringing inland with it the

*flat cries of a few lazy seagulls. The moment was over. His wise
counsellor had gone. As he drove home, slowly and mechanically,
like a man in a trance, Paddy was so absorbed in reliving the conversation that he forgot to stop for his few midday pints. Just as
well, he decided. Mick and Seán would think he was losing his
marbles if he told them what was going on in his head these days.*

About Dreaming

*Paddy was waiting in his office after school to interview a new
caretaker. The local priest dropped in. If the pastor hadn't looked
at his watch toward the end of their conversation, Paddy would
have asked him about dreams. He had recently begun to remember
his dreams and someone had told him to write them down because
it was very important to take notice of them. Paddy knew that this
new awareness of his dreams was linked with the general tumult
going on in his life, with his amazing conversations with Patrick,
and with the many feelings that kept churning inside him these
days. There was one dream in particular that remained vivid. It
had come two nights in a row. Before going to sleep, Paddy had
asked for guidance; he had prayed in some kind of way to some
kind of God for reassurance and encouragement during this
strange time in his life.*

*Later that evening, he again reviewed the dream. He was holding
a baby with his left arm. Suddenly the baby had become a small
girl whom he kissed. Looking him straight in the face she said 'Go
with the flow'. Immediately crowds of men came down the hillside
throwing stones at them. They also tried to block the road with big
rocks. Accurately, safely and very swiftly, the little girl directed
him along the winding roads, swaying in and out with perfect
judgment between the heaps of heavy stones. 'I wonder what it
means', Paddy mused drowsily as he lifted his feet onto a chair.
His head began to nod.*

Patrick: Your dreams are your friends. They only want to reveal to you your true self. Their aim is to complete your healing and your wholeness; to draw your attention to what is going on in the deepest part of you; to reach beneath the level of consciousness to the basic drives, desires and needs of your heart. In fact, in religious terms, it is said that God talks to us in a most creative and symbolic fashion in dreams.

Paddy: I never thought much about dreams or about what they might mean. How are they understood? Why are they so difficult to interpret?

Patrick: Every dream has many meanings. All the meanings are woven together into one story. This story is highly symbolic. Other people can help you in your search for the dream's meanings but no one can tell you its significance. Only you can determine that. It's like a flash of recognition from within that may only come after a long period of reflection. There is a moment when you may say, 'Ah, yes, that's it'; such a moment is the surest indication of your dream's meaning. It is a good idea to share your dreams with those who care about you deeply. Your dreams are quite sacred; they reveal more about you than you think. In fact very often, every character in your dream is a dimension of yourself.

The same dream narrative may carry elements of a recent event, personal sexual or childhood emotions, or may point to general human experiences. Contemporary students of dreams hold that these three dimensions are discernible in all dreams, together with some kind of tension or conflict between power and weakness, light and darkness.

Paddy: Will you interpret my dream for me?

Patrick: Only you can do that. I will help you to find the meaning that no one but you will recognise. Remember that the dream tries to clarify your life and your important relationships; it also recaptures elements of childhood. It is intuitive about the inevitability of death and, perhaps most of all, it works toward breakthrough and emotional rebirth by revealing something of the depths of ourselves we know so little about, especially our 'shadow side'.

Your dream is a beautiful one, full of wholeness and harmony. It is affirming and encouraging. The fact that it recurs is especially interesting. Try to link it with your other dreams and you may find a pattern emerging. In your dream, the baby on your left arm gently symbolises your inner child, the divine child of wonder within you. You are now more at ease in this relationship, increasingly in touch with your playfulness, your ability to trust, your openness, your awe at creation. The wounded child is healing and is ready to celebrate life because he is delighted with the way things are going for you. Does any of this make sense?

Paddy: You're touching chords now all right. Remarkable. Please keep going.

Patrick: The small baby girl in your dream represents the imaginative, intuitive, and tender dimensions of your personality. A man has such components in his make-up as well. But, because of pressure from society and the need, for various reasons, to establish a masculine image, these elements are often suppressed. These neglected components often appear in dreams in the shape of a woman. This 'inner female' the famous psychologist Carl Jung has termed 'the anima'. She is the lost other half of most men, a most important part of their soul. The *anima* plays a very important part in a man's relationships and can be an influence for rich growth or destructive imbalance.

The kiss given to the young girl, so clearly remembered by you, might mean the joyful meeting and befriending within you of the more tender, artistic, and wiser side of your deepest self. This side will bring you a new awareness of your power, an enriching wholeness where your emotions can be identified, named, owned, and expressed more appropriately. It would probably mean that you are becoming less defensive about admitting your pain and less embarrassed about showing it by grieving with words or tears. This kiss of life, in fact, symbolises for you your readiness to nourish this side of your personality by pursuing activities that engender within you words, thoughts, and inspirations of great beauty.

Paddy: This is great. Keep going. She spoke to me. 'Go with the flow', she said. What do you make of that?

Patrick: The baby, the girl, and the words are all connected. The four words are all about trusting your heart; they are about calling you out of your mind and encouraging you to come to your senses, urging you to be less cerebral and wordy, and more spontaneous and creative. The mystic within is aware of love as a gentle but powerful river whose waters bring healing, health of heart, visions of beauty, promises of ecstasy, and life from death. 'Go with the flow' reassures you that it's safe for you to trust the river, to believe in God.

Paddy: When you talk this way I think I can find some meaning in Christianity. You seem to be describing a kind of salvation from depression, a kind of resurrection from feeling lost. I suppose I'm experiencing now what could be called an amazing grace—a new creation in a way. But anyway, there's still the last part of the dream to be discussed, the bit about the men with the stones.

Patrick: You remember what I said about a threefold meaning in a dream narrative. The first level, a fairly obvious connection, could have been triggered by the sight of a group of workmen in a quarry near the airport yesterday afternoon. The second level, symbolised by the men with the stones, could refer to the resistance within you to experience true freedom. This seems to be a contradiction—a mysterious reluctance to be healed. The unwillingness to be guided out of our prison could be connected with humanity's strange history of persecuting its saviours. Throughout the evolving story of the universe, there is a recurring motif: the strange, shadow side of our personalities prompts us to assault those who bring good news about a new, free, and peaceful way of living. This would be the third level of interpretation. The New Testament is full of stories about men who stoned their liberators. Eventually, on a fateful weekend in Jerusalem, it relates how we killed the most beautiful and liberating man of all.

The most significant revelation I notice in this part of the dream involves our resistance to the necessary and crucial changes in our lives. Theologians sometimes refer to this mysterious human trait in terms of original sin. Men deny their need to change. They fail to recognise how stuck they are, and stubbornly refuse to be more communicative of their feelings. They mock the notion of the wounded child; they ridicule any suggestion to acknowledge and befriend what we described as their *anima*. This conflict is within us all: I fear both the beauty and the darkness within. I fear the call to freedom which might entail too much responsibility, too great a disturbance of my security. And how do I know where it will all end? Why take risks and be different? Why rock the boat and draw attention to myself? 'So settle for your lot', many say. 'There are others far worse off than you. Change is dangerous'. The temptation is to stay closed.

The dream ends so well. The female figure—your *anima*—to whom you are entrusting your immediate future is outwitting the attackers. The divine current of maternal creativity flows on, with speed, direction, and fulfillment. This dream is a delightful affirmation of your wonderful growth and the guarantee of an extraordinary and very tender presence in your life.

Paddy slowly awoke, and his mind drifted to the applicant for the caretaker's position. He reflected on the various meanings of the word 'caretaker'. What a lovely word. But it could describe someone who was a compulsive worrier about others. People imprisoned in this role were often reduced to being martyrs, victims and blamers. They needed a way out from the vicious circle of guilt and fear. Such 'caretakers' must learn to say 'no', he mused, they must learn to let go of their false sense of responsibility. Perhaps 'care-giver' was a healthier description. He looked at his watch and shook his head.

About Children

Paddy wasn't out of the woods yet. Sometimes he was flying high with a new freedom and suddenly he would be grounded by a stray shot of wild memory or confused by a passing cloud of grief. Tonight, lying awake again, he was feeling guilty about his neglect of the children. So often he would come home from school, watch television, read the paper, or go to the pub. He could have been a better father; he was usually too busy or too tired to spend time with them. He certainly did not love them unconditionally. He pushed them hard to study, kept them in at night when their peers were out, discouraged them from forming special relationships—just as he had been treated when he was their age.

Paddy tried to escape from this downward spiral of self-accusation. He realised he was being hard on himself. Maybe he had done the best he could, given the circumstances. Maybe his remorse was unfounded. Parents are not perfect. And it was never too late to learn. At least he could change his attitude now with the students in the school; he could encourage and affirm them more, praise them always for trying, celebrate their achievements.

One aspect of teaching that Paddy was beginning to enjoy was the time spent on creative writing. On Sunday evenings he carefully read and made written comments on students' essays. (He now had a pint before lunch on a Sunday and stayed home in the evening.) He was becoming increasingly critical of educational trends that led to cramming and performance, points and places. A year ago he had supported these. Children, he now felt, were being damaged by pressure and expectations at home and in school. They were being labelled as winners or losers.

'The yard behind the house where she used to sit and say the rosary isn't so green any more', wrote an eleven-year-old whose grandmother had just died out on her farm, 'but yesterday when I saw the new lambs playing, I knew she hadn't really died'. Paddy was moved. He was remembering his own anxious confusion and blocked understanding on the occasion, long ago, of his grandfather's burial. He rejoiced in this child's natural wisdom. He felt stirring within him a new, clear, and conscious passion to protect the original vision of children, to nourish their creativity, and to share this new excitement of his with their parents. As he drifted to sleep, he found himself engaged in yet another imaginary conversation with Patrick.

Patrick: Do not blame yourself for neglecting your children. You loved them so much. You worried about them; you provided for them materially. Do you remember the bedtime stories you told them? Some of them went on for weeks.

Don't punish yourself either about your educational views. After all, you did achieve excellent academic results. You devoted all your energies to becoming the best teacher around.

Paddy: But at what price? I nearly ruined my own life and those of the students. There was open competition and rivalry among them. That is destructive teaching. I saw knowledge as a possession to be acquired, the idea being to have more of it than the others, to obtain better results. The fear of failure, then, causes depression and low self-esteem. I can see this in myself, in other teachers, and in the way that students develop. Some personalities are being wounded, especially the older ones. It seemed to be different when I was at school. We were more of a happy family then; there was more fun and a greater sense of community.

Patrick: You remember the spirit of those days. A strong bond existed among parents, teachers and pupils. That is the way it should still be. Learning and teaching is meant to be a growing together in searching and sharing. Like midwives to each other, teachers and pupils draw out the child of imagination already within each one. Ideally, knowledge is seen as a gift and a grace to be humanised into a loving wisdom. There is a spontaneity and a dynamism in shared projects in which everyone's gifts and talents are valued and respected, especially those of the awkward or the slow. God's image shines in all children.

Paddy: I can assure you it wasn't always easy to find God's image in my own two children. But you are right. Only now can I see the sanctity of children. We can learn from their trust and openness. They love to play and they are usually delighted to be themselves. I often think how ironic it is that I, who find it so hard to forgive, tried to teach and explain this virtue to small children who are effortless and natural exponents of this divine grace. As a parent and teacher, I now regret my failure to revere the mystery of children. In a way, they are like God's dream come to life. They are full of innate justice and wisdom. You have helped me to see this, and also how they are wounded so deeply when we are careless with their feelings and hasty with our judgments.

I'm convinced now that delicate spirits are often crushed at root, and maybe crippled for life, through thoughtless and relentless negative criticism and comparisons from parents. I can remember, also, as a child, how evil I felt after some well-intentioned but dangerously misleading sermons.

Patrick: Yes, we have already talked about some of the effects of such wounds in later life. But I have also heard more enlightened parents and teachers discuss how best to liberate children's imagination through movement, drama, story, and the creative arts, releasing their sense of play, of worship, of creativity, of celebration. This is not all one-way traffic—the parent giving and the child receiving; the teacher, a full container, and the child, an empty vessel.

Children are not passive recipients. They are givers too. Parents and teachers are, in turn, empowered by drawing energy from the children. Adults are often healed by being open to their life-force. Notice how a baby can change many hearts. There is a saving power in children, in their simplicity, vulnerability, and readiness to grow.

Paddy: I believe there's a lot in what you're saying, and I'm beginning to agree with your whole approach. I'm still very much aware, however, of the potential for violence and destruction in all children.

Patrick: There is always the shadow-side of each person's spirit to be acknowledged and confronted. Our capacity for inhuman and subhuman behaviour is indeed a mystery. There are many learned attempts to explain why we do awful things, why we destroy what we love, why we are drawn toward demonic things. One fact we do know is that nearly all the callous crimes of these times are linked to a severly wounded childhood. This link has come up in many of our conversations. The emergence of cruel behaviour in children is, like that of the adult, most often caused by, and certainly accelerated by, lack of love, negative criticism, adult cynicism and ridicule, betrayed confidentiality, and inappropriate competitiveness. This inevitably leads to low self-esteem and high self-hatred.

Paddy: Does original sin come into this somewhere?

Patrick: I think it does. Each person is born with a readiness for contributing to the evil that already abounds. Why this is so remains a mystery. Where does this strange, sinister attraction toward the forces of destruction come from? We don't know, but we do know that the light is stronger than the darkness, that the energy of love outlasts the forces of fear. True education acknowledges this. It appeals to the seed of God in every child, to the fountain of the Holy Spirit that is always welling up in every heart, but uniquely in the young. This is the divine springtime that greens even the most arid soul.

Paddy: So it is important to affirm and celebrate the inherent goodness of children while remaining aware of the sleeping devils that inhabit all our hearts.

Patrick: There is a power for good in praising and encouraging all genuine effort and application. The aim is to be sensitive to all creative efforts. These efforts signal the expression of the child's divine image. Parents and teachers can trust the graced intuition of young hearts, encouraging a love for pluriformity and universality. Children are not racist or sexist or exclusivist in any innate way. They are to be protected from all false prejudices and narrow perspectives.

Paddy: I can see why I'm becoming disenchanted with my preferred model of teaching—the model that is suspicious of change. This approach falls in with current establishment expectations; it is product-oriented and functional. I was all for it.

There is a reluctance to move outside the system, to challenge structures, to acknowledge the weaknesses of yesterday's principles, to question curriculum content, teaching methods, and traditional exam procedures. In this model, pupils are regarded as potential adults, rather than as persons in their own right. There is a control and a predictability and therefore a fragmentation of knowledge and knowing. I now carry a deep fear of any kind of education that leads a student to become closed—closed as I have been over the decades.

Patrick: You are in good company. Many visionary educators hold that true teaching is basically about how to be open and how to stay that way. The openness is to the mystery of truth. And mystery is many-sided; therefore there will be a readiness for alternatives. The only worthy aim is ultimate freedom: for the child, for the community, for the world. It is the aim of the finest teachers in every generation.

You mentioned the necessity of seeing children as complete persons, so complete that we must all become like them if we are to get to heaven. Education, I think, is about the *present* nourishing and developing of the emotions for *now*, as well as of the cognitive faculties for the future, in a holistic curriculum. It is about relationships and choices, about the building up of self-esteem, about spiritual growth, about nurturing the desire to learn with others, about deepening trust, respect, and wisdom, about revering the original vision at the heart of every child.

Paddy: What kind of world do you think will result from such a model of education?

Patrick: The world, I feel sure, is on the brink of a unique transformation. The twilight of the second millennium will see, I sense, the end of humanity's adolescence. After a bloody century of unbelievable irresponsibility and unprecedented madness, during which we have all but destroyed our mother earth and her human family, there are unmistakeable signs of a healing network of love spreading across the world. Today's children will be the architects and sustainers of this world come of age. That is why their education will be toward justice, compassion, freedom, and peace. It will be about quality of life for each person, for all people, and for the cosmos itself. It will be about issues of exploitation of the poor and of the earth, about consumerism, militarism, and all forms of manipulation and oppression.

If empowered by a heart-centred and creation-conscious model of education, today's children, already vibrant with God's energy and love, will outgrow our adult fascination with war, with boundaries, with flags, with fear. They will create an option for openness and trust between hearts and between countries, breaking down the familiar cynicism and suspicion that breeds anxiety. They will believe in love. In God's strange economy, they will be the young artisans of a new age, the unlikely prophets of our present time, the saviours of an old world.

Paddy fell into a deep sleep. He had a lovely dream. It was of a world ruled by boys and girls. Many of them were handicapped. It was a kind of Camelot existence, where peace and justice flourished and there was much play and laughter. Adults were listening intently to the children. Very old people were in deep and private communication with babies. Animals, insects, and birds were congregating in groups everywhere. All the humans were bare-

foot. What was so striking about the whole scene was the absence of fear. No one was afraid because there was no danger or rumour of danger. Where there is no pain, there is perfect trust.

About Intimacy

Now that Paddy's life was renewed and the true beauty of his spirit was emerging, he was experiencing many strong emotions. These were not like the 'highs' he would get after a good few drinks, or the 'lows' he had after being beaten at squash or being at the wrong end of an argument with a teacher or parent. These new feelings were somehow more intangible, deeper, and more elusive. And it wasn't as though they were completely new. They were, in fact, vaguely familiar. It was as though he was meeting childhood friends after a long absence. These moments of strange intensity were happening to him more often now. One evening his daily walk took him farther than he had intended. He took a short-cut home through the fields. As he clambered over a mossy stone-wall he noticed a perfect wild flower, an Oxeye daisy, breathtakingly white against the dark green. An aching sensation embraced him, of loneliness and longing, but of warmth and joy too. It was like a memory that blessed and burned—a memory that seemed to go back before his time on this earth....

Patrick: What's happening to you is not unusual. You are reclaiming the love of nature you had as a boy. Lots of people experience these moments. For many reasons, however, they rarely talk about them. They are very special glimpses of God's beauty, of where we have come from and where we are going. They are reminders of our true nature and our true homeland. They warn us about settling for less along the way, about believing that we are less than divine. We come from God, we are full of God, and we are destined to be transformed fully into God. Ecstatic as the beauty and loveliness of our experiences of creation and of creatures may be, they are still pointing toward the source of all beauty and pleasure: the tremendous divine lover. Your mystical moment with the wild flower, like in your childhood relationship with your grandfather, was a small sacrament of the intimacy that already exists between your own beauty and the spirit of nature, an intimacy that will one morning be completely fulfilled in God's own heart. The evening of your death to separation here will be the morning of your birth to intimacy with beauty in what we call heaven.

Paddy: But in that moment at the stonewall, everything was so unbelievably perfect; everything was in deep harmony, shining and flowing like a river of lights. What does it all mean?

Patrick: For a fleeting moment, the veil was lifted and you were blessed among women and men. They say that, if we could see things as they really are, we would be blinded by the loveliness of creation. The wisest scholars and the holiest saints have told us that a grain of sand, a blade of grass, a drop of water are all so mysteriously made that if we could understand them we would understand God. There are people who can see with their hearts and their vision of beauty and of pain is intense and moving. They see below the surface of things; they touch the shining river of lights that connects all of life. They experience an intimacy with the mountains and the trees, with the birds and animals, with children and with adults. Unlike the rest of us, they have not allowed the barriers to be built up around their hearts. They have avoided addictions and distracting detours. The unerring, homing instinct of their hearts has been trusted to bring them to a true intimacy with the love that is the source of life. Our spirit is restless until it rests with the spirit of God.

This, I think, is what these small but profound epiphanies are about, and your grandfather forty years ago, along with most children, are graced with such epiphanies. These fleeting revelations, these windows of wonder, remind us of our true nature, so agonisingly lovely, and of the unity and intimacy of spirit that flows between all things.

Paddy: Are you saying that we are attracted toward loveliness and beauty because we are made in the image of God, who is love and beauty? That our desire for intimacy with what is beautiful here on earth is part of a desire for the beauty which is infinite? That all our truly human loving is God's delighted loving going on in us, and between ourselves and nature?

Patrick: I am. You have put it very clearly. The world is God's body. All ground is holy ground. All water is holy water. Every mountain is a sacred mountain. Every new birth is a beautiful new face of God. Apart from evil, there is no place that is not filled with eternal love. In God we live and move and have our being.

But we get confused. We are often misled. We are sidetracked. Yet the quest is never abandoned. In fact, everything we do is part of the search. That search sometimes goes terribly wrong and at those times God shares our anguish at the evil that happens. But all hearts are created in God's image and are therefore always deeply loved. That is why we long for unity with love, for intimacy with the spirit of beauty; that is why our relationships are so important to us, why we pray, why we get married. Our very nature, in its incompleteness, yearns for completion. One of the clearest examples of this tremendous attraction is human sexuality.

Paddy: Could you say more about sexuality and intimacy?

I'm a little anxious these years about being less interested in the physical side of our marriage. But I'm aware recently too of a deeper kind of loving with Eileen; a kind of intimacy, I suppose, that wasn't there before.

Patrick: The deepest human need is intimacy, not sex. Intimacy is about total trust in the fact that I am known and loved by another even as I, in turn, know and trust. To be whole and to experience peace we all need intimacy in some fashion. People are often confused about this passion for intimacy with someone because it is often first experienced by young men as the physical sex drive. These two needs, for intimacy and for sexual gratification, often stay unconnected, with very regrettable consequences. It is so important to be able to distinguish between the two. When experienced together, when each is the appropriate expression of the other, they combine to create one of the most powerful moments of all. There is no need for you to be anxious. What you describe so honestly is common enough for men in mid-life, especially if much of their energy is also being channelled into other ways of being creative and of growing spiritually.

Paddy: I suppose that you'll be saying next that sexuality is bound up with spirituality?

Patrick: Our sexuality is always bound up with our spirituality. My relationship with God is inseparably connected to my relationship with others. They are both expressions of the same drive toward intimacy. Both are full of grace and passion, desire, commitment and fidelity. While our spirituality is a very earthy reality, our sexuality is empowered by divine grace. It is a sacrament of God's desire that we should all be one. It is a symbol of the longing for unity and completion at the heart of all creation. But our sexuality needs to be healed. Suppressed and damaged in a wounded childhood as our sexuality is, further distortion and disorientation happen through involvement in the unavoidable sin of the world. Nevertheless, in spite of the shadows that fall across this most fragile gift, human sexuality is God's love incarnate in our hearts and bodies, as the vulnerable, joy-filled setting for divine ecstasy to happen on earth when we co-create with God. So there is nothing wrong in believing that we honour God in our sexuality. Through this blessing and grace we experience another unique revelation of God's extravagant love for us.

Paddy: Well, they never put it that way when I was learning the catechism! But, thanks to you, I'm beginning to see things quite differently now from some of the fear-filled ways I saw them in the past. And yet, even though no one told me before about the lovely things we have discussed—about beauty and childhood, about trusting and healing, about sexuality and intimacy, about an extraordinarily compassionate God—in some mysterious way I have known them already, not with my head but with my heart. Thank you; your work is done, but stay close!

It occurred to Paddy, as he continued on his way home, that he had begun separating himself defensively at a very early age, as most males do, first from his mother and then from females in general. He could now identify a kind of fear he had of women, even a hidden disdain, in order to protect his 'maleness'. This fear led also to a disowning of his anima because of the intimacy it implied—an intimacy that could undermine the separation on which his male identity was founded. 'How complex and intricate', Paddy mused in wonder, 'are the webs we weave deep in our souls'.

Epilogue: Paddy and Eileen

Paddy's personal transformation was now well underway. Like a dry riverbed, he had been ready for flooding once the blockage of twisted and knotted debris that had formed earlier upstream had been broken through. Surging with free-flowing life, he was a new man. Currently he enjoyed organising adult education classes on creative hobbies two evenings a week in the school for the local parents. Seán jokingly referred to him as the new 'patron of the arts'. He sometimes missed the company of the lads and the nightly pints. But they met every Sunday after Mass to catch up on the news. Paddy had also agreed to go with Eileen and Peggy to an introductory course on how to acquire skills in counselling. 'Here comes Kerry's answer to Mr Freud' was Mick's current greeting each Sunday. He walked a few brisk miles every day and often dropped in for a satisfying chat with Father Brian whenever he passed the church. He had met Brian after Benediction that first night in the church. They had long since unearthed the traumatic experience with the 'hell-fire missioner' of his childhood days, and a gradual reconciliation with the institutional church was under way.

Paddy had certainly broken through. This new awareness, however, was making him sensitive to unaccustomed issues. His second journey brought a deep and personal concern about the political, economic, and religious state of his country. Without really trying, he felt a close bond with all people and all creation. Just as his external lifestyle had cleaned itself up through discipline regarding his health, order in his daily duties, pride in his professional life, and awareness where his emotions were concerned, so too with his social consciousness. He now realised how closed he had been, how domestic were his interests, how parochial was his sense of responsibility. He had never taken really seriously the pain of the world's oppressed: the suffering of political prisoners, the plight of refugees, the anger of the dispossessed, the powerless-

ness of the poor and hungry, the mindless mutilation of beautiful Mother Earth.

This evening he was watching yet another documentary on Northern Ireland with Eileen. His spirits were down as the cruelty of human beings to one another and to the earth itself swept over him. What insidious spirit of evil resides in the human heart? he wondered. What devils run wild in our souls without warning? Why do we so love our games of war, our violence and sexism even in the name of patriotism and religion? Why are we so afraid of the stranger, of those who are different?

Eileen was sensing his mood. In recent times they had moved closer to each other—a blessing they scarcely could have hoped for, a gift and grace that brought profound joy.